BEYOND THE LESSON PLANS

Six Keys to Unlocking the Potential of All Students

BY: CLAYTON PAUL THOMAS

M.A.T. in Elementary Education

This publication is designed to provide competent and reliable information regarding the subject matter covered. However, it is sold with the understanding that the author and publisher are not engaged in rendering legal or other professional advice. If expert assistance is required, a professional should be sought. The author specifically disclaims any liability that is incurred from the use or application of the contents in this book.

Printed by CreateSpace

First printing: December 2013

ISBN-13: 978-1-4895-1628-2
ISBN-10: 1-4895-1628-X

This book is dedicated to all of the hardworking staff of Portland Elementary and Bates Elementary in Louisville, Kentucky. The effort and time you have placed into those wonderful students will never be forgotten.

To my beautiful wife, Lauren, who has blessed me with her love since the early days of St. Joseph Children's Home.

She has stuck with me throughout all of the lessons I have learned about children and hope to teach in this book.

Thanks so much for being there.

I love you.

CONTENTS

PREFACE...I

CHAPTER 1 1
Classroom Discipline Starts with the Person in Charge

CHAPTER 2..19
Understanding the Troubled Child

CHAPTER 3..31
All Learning Starts with Motivation

CHAPTER 4 47
The Expectation Attitude

CHAPTER 5..55
Circling the Educational Wagons

CHAPTER 6 65
Pulling the Educational Bandwagon Outside of the Box

FINAL THOUGHTS..75

APPENDIX A 79

APPENDIX B...81

PREFACE

Beyond the Lesson Plans is a book for teachers and prospective teachers who want to maximize the academic potential of all students. As a classroom teacher, I have worked with many fine professionals through the years who wanted only the best for their students. Year after year, however, test scores would be released, and they would never be as high as any of us would have liked. Scores in some academic areas would go up, whereas others went down. The following year, the trend would reverse completely.

The teachers I worked with, like you, were proud people. They really wanted test scores to reflect the hard work they put into the students. When this didn't happen, there were various levels of blame, frustration, and self-doubt. These frustrations may have been directed toward the administration, parents, the tests, or even the students themselves.

Although testing seems beneficial, I wish tests were not used as the scorecard for modern education. The fact remains that student performance on standardized tests is the basis for judging our nation, our states, our cities, our schools, and even our teachers. Besides, even teachers who are not ardent fans of testing would still like to see children do well on tests and benefit from the other advantages education has to offer.

So many issues can influence test scores and overall student performance, some of which teachers can control, whereas others are more difficult. This book strategically dissects the elements of education that teachers can control. Strategies in each chapter demonstrate how to tackle those elements with the goal of maximizing student performance.

For example, I delve deeply into working with students who have behavior problems. I started my career by working at an inner city school that had its fair share of student behavior problems. Early on, it became apparent that behavior issues had to be limited and, ultimately, eliminated before a teacher could get into a rhythm with his or her class. A teacher's job is not, however, merely to make a child behave. A teacher's job is to educate all students, regardless of race, gender, socioeconomic conditions, or parental participation.

After showing how to establish the rhythm of the class, I address how to work with students in order to maximize their educational potential. Important life events can happen to children over the course of a school year, however, that typically disrupt learning. Therefore, I discuss the three big events I found as a teacher and how I handled each one.

Next, I address what I have found to be the number one key to student achievement: motivation. A motivated child is one who works hard, even when the material is challenging; therefore, this book provides seven motivational tactics that I use with success. Although it can be difficult for any student to be motivated every day for nine months, these strategies will assist teachers significantly in this endeavor.

Teacher expectations are addressed in the next chapter. For years, I was instructed to have high expectations of students and myself. The concept, however, was always vague to me. Does it mean that everyone should get an A in every class? Should all students ace their standardized tests? If that did not happen, did it mean that my expectations were not high enough? The crux of the matter is how high expectations should be judged and who should do the judging.

After establishing the foundation in the first four chapters, I dedicate my efforts to showing how teachers can accomplish more collectively than individually. Teachers, despite their best efforts, cannot be everywhere in the classroom at once. Therefore, my contention is that in order to get maximum results from students, the community must be involved to give individual attention to the students who would most benefit from it. From there, the book discusses strategies for getting high-octane volunteers in the schools.

Technology and internet based learning are the final topics in the book but certainly not the least important. These topics can be overwhelming due to the amount of content that exists. Therefore, I go into full details as to which websites teachers should be using now and why it will pay dividends.

Depending on where you are in your educational journey, you may already be implementing some of the ideas discussed in this book. Other ideas, however, may seem a bit overwhelming. No matter where you are in your career, I hope you will read this book with an open mind and a critical ear. It is up to you as the classroom teacher to decide what you are going to do with the material here.

Whether you try to tackle all the strategies presented or use only a few, please know that I am cheering for you. I have walked in your shoes, and I know the difficulties of the job. I wish you the best of luck on your educational journey!

CHAPTER 1

Classroom Discipline Starts with the Person in Charge

All educators have strengths and weaknesses. I have worked with many teachers who have been brilliant in terms of lesson planning, organization, and time management, but some of those same teachers were not good with discipline. Their lack of classroom discipline, consequently, marginalized everything else they were good at. The good news is that things can change rapidly. For the good of the students, having strong classroom management skills must become a priority.

One of the most productive things to do when attempting to deal with a disruptive student is to determine the root cause of the disruption. The quickest answer will usually be discovered by the teacher. A classroom educator controls approximately six hours of a child's day, roughly thirty hours per week. That is plenty of time to know why a child is acting out and to come up with concrete strategies to deal with the issue.

Some teachers of disruptive children are going to point to parents as the cause because they are raising the child improperly (in their eyes) or point to the administration because they do not "do enough" when a teacher sends a child to the office. Therefore, let us address these issues. Although the teachers' opinions may have a lot of validity, teaching, in today's culture, is a results-oriented business. If a teacher goes into a classroom with an attitude that certain children cannot learn based on their behavior, odds are the teacher is correct. Consequently, a teacher may subconsciously lower his or her expectations not only for the troubled student, but also for the class. The attitude would look something like this: *If only I didn't have that troublemaker, Bobby, in my class, everyone else would learn so much more.* The thing is that nearly all teachers have challenging students. How teachers deal with those challenges ultimately determines the success of the class.

Here is a story from many years ago that still irks me to this day. At one of my former grade schools, I had a good reputation for being a disciplinarian. It was common for other teachers to send discipline problems to me. What wound up happening is that when a new school year began, I received a disproportionate number of these behavior problems because of my abilities.

Our second grade team of teachers gave a reading assessment to uncover strengths and weaknesses of students. Though the scores were similar overall, my class results were a little poorer. At first, I was upset because my class didn't do better. The principal sent a shot across my bow that sounded something like this: *Clayton, you know you are going to have to improve these scores.* He said it in a tone to put me down in front of my colleagues. Although I knew I wanted my students to improve, I also remembered that the classes were not divided evenly in terms of ability. I had the lower-performing children with the discipline problems.

The next day, I went into the classroom with a focused attitude. I lectured to my students for several minutes on being the best class in the entire school and how we were going to accomplish it. Although they were small children, these youngsters were hanging on my every word. It was unfortunate that our grade level wasn't given a follow-up test because I wanted the challenge. That group of behaviorally challenged students wound up being one of many great classes I was proud to teach.

The most important thing any teacher can do in the beginning of the school year is to set the tone.

Teachers are responsible for creating a learning environment in their classrooms, and that starts on day one. Some teachers set the tone for their classrooms by having the students create a list of rules for the classroom. More of the environment, however, comes simply from the attitude of the person running the classroom.

In my last book for parents called *Tantrums, Troubles, and Treasures,* I discussed a gentleman named Eric, whose story is useful here. Eric worked with me at St. Joseph Children's Home in Louisville, Kentucky, a home for children who had been separated from their parents by the courts because of some form of physical, sexual, or emotional abuse. In other words, when a child walked through the door at St. Joseph's, he or she carried a lot of baggage. Our job, as house parents, was to work through the problems created through the children's previous environments. Our goal was to prepare them for future settings while giving them the love they did not receive at home. The best-case scenario for these children was adoption, but many were placed in great foster homes.

There are many stories about Eric in the book, but the point I want to relay is this: when Eric walked into a room, he commanded respect from children. It didn't matter what had happened during the prior shift or the previous day. Children knew to be on their best behavior. Working with him was always a pleasure because the residents behaved beautifully. Consequently, they had a lot more fun with one another because of the way he set the tone. I learned a lot from Eric, but his presence alone solved problems before they even started. I replicated his no-nonsense approach in my classroom with great success.

In my classrooms, I set the tone just like all teachers. The tone and general demeanor a teacher exhibits go a long way in determining how students behave. The tone of any classroom is based on many things. Here are some examples.

TONE OF VOICE

Teachers have to be aware of their voice levels. For example, children in the back of the classroom have to be able to hear you clearly. It is also important, though, not to appear to be shouting to the students in the front. For this reason, it is important for teachers to move around the room as much as possible when they are teaching. Also, teachers have to be aware of their tone around students during transitional periods. For example, children get excited before lunch and may not listen as well as during other times. I found that using the sound of a small bell grabbed the attention of students without having to raise my voice.

The teachers' tone is also important when dealing with discipline issues. It is important for teachers to use a tone that is authoritative and controlled. I have witnessed several teachers struggle with students. One reason is that their voice level was not controlled. When a teacher's voice level goes up, that subconsciously tells some students that they must raise their voice level in order to be heard. Teachers need to avoid this escalation of voices.

TEACHERS' DRESS

The way a teacher dresses goes a long way in determining how seriously students will take him or her. I wore dress slacks and a collared shirt every day. The one exception to my professional dress was my shoes. I wore tennis shoes because I moved around a lot in the classroom and played games at recess with the students.

I worked with some women who occasionally wore T-shirts or skirts that were too far above the knee, projecting an image that made it difficult for students to take them seriously in the classroom. Teaching is a serious profession. The successful teachers I worked with always dressed professionally.

BODY LANGUAGE

Teachers have to remember to keep a bounce in their step and a smile on their faces as much as possible. Students are great at picking up on indications that you are not excited to be there and ready to teach. The moment they notice negative body language, they set up barriers to learning. Material must be presented in an upbeat manner.

Body language was also important for me beyond the general curriculum. I assumed that children were always watching me. Therefore, how I conducted myself around other teachers, the administration, and students I was disciplining from other classrooms was important. In terms of the students from other classrooms, I was one of a handful of teachers students were sent to in order to cool down. All teachers are role models. How teachers conduct themselves in the face of students could be mimicked at a separate time or place. Therefore, teachers who display confidence in who they are and what they are teaching typically have fewer problems than someone who is so friendly that they forget the task at hand which is educating all students. Body language had a lot to do with why I was trusted to work with students who needed to cool down.

When I was teaching, I did not focus on a student's home life between 9:15 a.m. and 3:45 p.m. because I was too busy educating students and setting a proper tone. When any child entered my classroom, he or she was in my world, and it was not run like a democracy. As a teacher, I was there solely to teach, and my students had better be there solely to learn. I strove every day to have a presence like Eric's. If a child's home life is bad enough to cause his or her behavioral problems, then you as the classroom teacher should be the highlight of his or her day.

HAVE A SOLID GAME PLAN

One of the reasons students disrupt classrooms is that they are not engaged at the level teachers need them to be. When looking through the lesson plans, teachers should always be thinking beyond the lesson. Specifically, they should be thinking about the overall class dynamic and what complications could arise with a lesson due to disruptions or a lack of understanding. For example, some students disrupt lessons when they are not feeling adequate to do the work or when concepts go over their heads (they get bored). Knowing this, I may have the student next to me as I am teaching the lesson, or I may place a brighter student next to my troubled one. I would use the student trick only if that bright student was outgoing and engaging. Quiet students who are bright usually do not benefit children who have behavior problems. Although the opposite gender could be used in certain circumstances, I would normally prefer that the more advanced student be the same gender as the child who misbehaves.

The worst thing a teacher can do for students who cause trouble is give them time to let their minds wander. When troubled children are engaged, they are much less likely to think about causing mischief.

Teachers should remember that lesson plans aren't just about planning the lesson itself. Lesson planning should be focused on the knowledge garnered after teaching the lesson. This means that every child (especially the troubled student) has to be engaged in order to receive the maximum benefit from the lesson. When thinking about each lesson in this way, the teacher will see an increase in the workload, but then again the test scores will also increase.

Teachers sometimes must adjust the game plan if children have to work in groups. Again, in this situation, a child's mind can wander. Teachers should place children who can cause trouble in groups rather than allowing them to choose their group, which often invites disaster, especially if the teacher has to focus on another group. The question at hand should be this: When the students go into groups, where is the most likely place little Bobby can succeed? In the end, a teacher may determine that, based on his behavior, little Bobby is not ready for a group. A teacher may have to work with little Bobby individually. Success does not always involve fairness. It is about maximizing the abilities of all children.

What frequently happens is that little Bobby doesn't want to be singled out. At this point, a teacher has a leveraging tool. A teacher's response is simple: *You can go over to that group (again the teacher chooses the group), but if I catch you not trying your best, I bet you know what will happen.* " I have used this tactic many times. Would you believe I never had to move a behaviorally challenged child back by himself or herself?

* * *

Knowing which students might cause trouble by talking with their previous teachers has always been helpful to me. In the case of a kindergarten teacher, there's nothing wrong with calling a preschool to see if there is anything of which you should be made aware. This doesn't mean I am going to profile a child or even assume that a previous teacher is correct in his or her assessment. It simply gives me a starting point, which every teacher needs. If teachers have to figure out everything on their own and take a month to do it, valuable class time is already lost.

An old adage I heard at the beginning of every year states that a teacher should be strict at the beginning of the year and then loosen up as the year moves on. This advice is simply not true. Contrarily, a teacher needs to be consistent from day one in order to keep all students focused. When any child loses his or her focus, academic and behavioral problems can occur.

When—not if—there is a child you feel may be a challenge, you should already have a plan. My favorite things to do with disruptive students include the following:

1. Sit them in the front of the room or between members of the opposite gender, depending on the classroom layout. **Note: This solution doesn't always work with older students who may be "dating." A teacher has to have his or her finger on the pulse of these situations.** Generally speaking, though, a proper seating arrangement sets the tone. You are already on to the antics of that child, and seating the child apart from his or her friends sends a powerful message. Doing it in the beginning of the school year also means the child is less likely to feel singled out.

2. Give disruptive students jobs. It's vital to keep busy hands busy. It also makes a student feel important. This fact cannot be overstated. When a student feels important, he or she is less likely to be disruptive. The counter to this would be that I was not being fair to all students because the jobs wouldn't be given equally. My response is simple. My job is not to be fair. It is for students to learn the most they can from me in the time we have together.

COMMUNICATE HIGH EXPECTATIONS

Chapter 4 deals exclusively with the expectation attitude. For now, though, let me just say that a teacher should establish in his or her mind what the term means and how it can help a struggling student.

Many teachers I have worked with have heard about high expectations for so long, they are almost numb to the term. Many people use it but seldom hear it defined. Before reading further, please take a few seconds to think about your definition of high expectations.

Here's my definition: *High expectations are achieved when teachers get their students to perform their best.*

You'll notice I didn't mention anything about grades or standardized test scores. That is because all students are not capable of getting a particular grade at a given time. For a variety of reasons, a child may not be ready to get an A on a report card. It could be, for example, that the previous teacher was not very good. The current teacher is now busy filling in the missing pieces of material the student should have already received. Perhaps with a little extra push, though, the child may be ready to get a higher grade on the next report card. If a teacher is pushing a child to do his or her best, good things will happen, even if it takes longer than we would like. Sometimes children have challenges. There is no shame in acknowledging those challenges, but teachers do students a disservice when they use those challenges as an excuse for students not to do their best. If the best a child can do on a test is a C, that grade should be celebrated, even if continued improvement is the goal.

Before a lesson begins, it is important to state the objectives of the lesson and communicate the desired outcomes. Stating objectives and outcomes would look something like this:

Today for math we are going to be learning about adding fractions with different denominators. If you don't understand how to do this by the end of the lesson, I will find a different way to teach you the concept. All of you will be expected to know the process of how to add these types of fractions and why adding fractions is important. Open your ears wide, and let's begin!

In this circumstance, having high expectations means a teacher has to plant the seeds of success to make the educational plant grow.

My example can be done in mere seconds, but taking those seconds to communicate the expectation to the students can go a long way. When a teacher fails to do this, mischievous students who are daydreaming may be on their way to causing trouble because they are already behind the eight ball on this particular lesson. One thing mischievous Bobby is typically good at is finding ways to fill in the time.

UNDERSTAND YOUR STRENGTHS AND WEAKNESSES

One of the keys to working with disruptive and underperforming students is for teachers to determine what they are really good at and what could be improved. Teachers have an incredible number of responsibilities, and it would be foolish to believe that all teachers are great at all aspects of teaching. Here is a checklist of things to consider, along with a guideline for grading. It would be a good idea for a teacher to fill out the checklist on his or her own. Afterwards, have your principal take a look at your evaluation and see if he or she agrees with your assessment. Some teachers may struggle with evaluating themselves, so don't overlook the valuable resource of a second opinion from your principal. This list is not meant to embarrass anyone. Receiving an A in all of these areas consistently would be highly challenging. But if a teacher doesn't understand his or her strengths and weaknesses, it is very difficult to improve. Colleagues and principals of teachers reading this book are encouraged to add to or improve upon this list based on the dynamics of their school and individual needs.

1. LESSON PLANNING

a) This grade would indicate that a principal could walk in, understand your plan, and implement it even if you are out sick. Clear goals and objective measures to be assessed are clearly laid out. Finally, a contingency plan would also address students who may potentially struggle with the lesson and the appropriate steps to take.

b) This grade would be given if the plan is clear to a principal. The goals of the lesson and the objective measures are written, but they could be more clearly defined. The lesson plan is still fairly solid, but it could be tightened up a bit. The contingency plans for students who do not understand are present.

c) This grade would be given to a teacher who has a plan a principal could follow but may be lacking a clear purpose. The goals and objectives of the lesson are too vague for students to understand. The contingency plan for students who do not understand is present but would not be easily understood by the principal. The overall lesson is difficult to implement properly to gain maximum educational success.

d) This grade would be given for a lesson plan that wouldn't be easy for a principal to follow. Goals and objective measures are not clearly defined. There also is not a contingency plan for students who don't understand the assignment.

e) Lesson plans are not clear for a principal to understand. There is not a clear direction in the lesson plan. Objective measures and a contingency plan for a struggling student do not exist.

2. DISCIPLINE

a) The teacher has few disruptions. When disruptions occur, the teacher can get the child reengaged with the lesson quickly. The tone of the room is clear in terms of who is in charge and what's going to happen on a particular day. Generally speaking, the same student does not disrupt the class. Students are engaged and excited about follow-up lessons. The teacher has a clear plan when misbehavior occurs. The teacher also demonstrates his or her options for disciplining students in a professional manner. Students know what is expected of them and are held accountable when they do not live up to those expectations.

b) The teacher experiences disruptions but handles them professionally. He or she can reengaged students with a lesson but not quite as quickly as an A disciplinarian. Students are generally engaged and excited to learn. The plan for redirecting when misbehavior occurs is not completely clear, though the teacher is attentive. The same student(s) tend to disrupt more than others but not to the point where class time has to be adjusted significantly. Teacher confidence and frustration is shaken occasionally when plan A for disciplining a child doesn't work. Students generally know what is expected and are held accountable most of the time.

c)   The teacher experiences disruptions. Reengaging a disruptive student proves to be difficult to the point where lessons have to be halted before the misbehavior is fully addressed. Students can be found in the counselor's or principal's office regularly. The teacher has signaled to the students that he or she does not have control. A discipline plan and accountability measures need to be enforced with better consistency.

d)   The teacher experiences weekly disruptions during lessons. Lessons have to be discontinued, and students are not reengaged after the misbehavior occurs. The misbehaving student staying quiet and out of the way is good enough for the teacher. The discipline plan and accountability measures are not being enforced. Learning is inhibited by lack of classroom control.

e)   The teacher experiences frequent chaos in the classroom. Lessons are consistently disrupted. Due to the disruptions, consistent learning is not taking place by the majority of students. The teacher has no discipline plan or accountability measures.

3. STUDENT ENGAGEMENT

a)   Students look forward to going to class because of the personality of the teacher and the creativity of the lessons. Measureable results are achieved and documented. Students raise their hands consistently during lessons. There is an action plan for students struggling with the content. Struggling students feel comfortable asking questions and receive the feedback necessary to solve any confusion with the content. Students who grasp the content receive extension assignments that are challenging and thought provoking.

b) Students generally like the teacher and like going to class. The lessons are tedious from time to time, but, overall, the teacher keeps a good pace. Measureable results are achieved and documented. The class is generally engaged. There is an action plan for students struggling with the content. Struggling students feel comfortable asking questions when prompted but won't initiate questions. Students who grasp the content earlier than others receive high grades, but extension assignments are inconsistent.

c) Students do not have a good connection with the teacher. Lessons are ordinary— most likely coming straight from a manual. A test may be given at the end of the unit, but a pretest is not given to see what students already knew. No action plan is in place other than a note to parents requesting they work on X. Struggling students generally do not ask questions. They stay quiet and watch the time pass. Students who grasp the content early participate but aren't challenged and will easily receive an A. These students are bored.

d) Students would rather not go to class based on the content and the teacher. Lesson pacing is typically an issue. Struggling students stay quiet. Students who already know the content will not be challenged and will easily receive their A. These students are bored.

e) Students are not engaged in the lesson or the teacher. They are in class physically but not mentally. Students generally do not raise their hands. There isn't an action plan for struggling students. Teachers rely on the strong performances from the gifted students to make them feel good about the overall lesson.

As you can see, making the highest grades isn't easy. Teaching isn't any different from other highly sought-after professions in the sense that one could easily work twenty-four hours a day and seven days a week. Because it is impossible to do this, the question then becomes where to draw the line when it comes to investing the time to improve. The teachers who put the extra time in and use their time most wisely are generally the ones who have better results. In other words, if you compared teachers on both ends of the educational spectrum, the teacher who puts the time in would produce a stronger class. This would be true even if the students from both classes were switched.

GAME PLAN FOR STRENGTHS AND WEAKNESSES

The way that I started my employment at St. Joseph Children's Home was much different from the way I started my teaching career. This distinction is important because there are certain elements of education we have to look at through a different lens in order to maximize teacher strengths and minimize any weaknesses.

At St. Joseph's, I worked with a team so that I was not alone with the children for very long. I had excellent people to guide and mentor me as well. From there, I was entrusted to another department by myself, but there were still staff members close by whom I could rely on in a time of need. The reason for the switch was that I was highly recommended by these staff members and through the observations from the administration. Because I sought the advice of house parents who knew more than I, they soon trusted me with greater responsibility. After more time, I was placed back in my original department. This time, though, I was more of a trainer for new staff. I had come full circle.

Teachers are not afforded the same luxury as I had at St. Joseph. This is important because teachers often do not have anyone to rely on in their time of need with a student other than simply sending him or her to the office. Obviously, when any child is sitting in the office, learning is not occurring. Bad habits can turn into the norm and then be repeated year after year. The best thing a teacher can do is to have constant communication with other staff and the administration when problems occur. Even if you are a 15 year veteran, it is possible that another teacher has had more success dealing with a difficult classroom situation that you are currently experiencing.

Teachers do not have a lot of time to figure out the teaching profession in the public school system and use class after class of students as their guinea pigs. Swallowing my pride at St. Joseph and asking tough questions was a benefit to me at St. Joseph and subsequently in the classroom. I believe that you will find the same to be true by relying on other staff members and the administration at your school.

Here are two steps that help maximize a teacher's strengths and weaknesses:

1. **Build Lesson-Planning Teams**: Most teachers work in horizontal (grade groups) and/or vertical teams (first, second, third grade), but this team may be different depending on the makeup of the staff. The idea entails, for example, pairing a teacher who could use some tweaking with his or her lesson-planning techniques with the best lesson planners in the build-

ing. Lesson-planning ideas for a given unit would be exchanged and implemented, addressing especially the higher- and lower-achieving students. The key to this step, though, is to have staff members willing to work with one another versus going through the motions. To get better at lesson planning, a teacher has to be able to admit when there is room to improve and be willing to take criticism constructively.

2. **Build a Discipline Team**: There should be a productive way for teachers to vent their frustrations and still get positive feedback. Teachers should team up with others who are strong disciplinarians to exchange ideas. The team should have serious conversations concerning, for example, what type of student behaviors are adversely affecting learning. Also, address what short-term and long-term steps need to be implemented. What are the conditions for removing the student from the classroom—and for how long?

3. Although involving a principal or counselor to remove a student can be part of the overall behavioral plan, please remember this: every minute a student is out of the classroom is another minute that could lead to a lower test score. Ironically, the better a teacher can do his or her job, the more the student is missing out. Discipline teams should come up with an action plan to keep students learning inside the classroom.

When reading this chapter, keep in mind that changes are not going to come overnight. It takes a lot of guts for teachers to admit things could be going better. And it takes a lot of courage and dedication to establish solid game plans. It is much easier for any teacher to go home and grade papers on his or her couch than to look in the mirror and contemplate how to get mischievous Bobby to perform at his optimal level.

Finally, remember that all teachers have strengths. Make sure you are there for others in their time of need. If you are good at planning lessons but poor at discipline, match up with someone who is poor at planning lessons and strong in discipline. These types of relationships will benefit the entire student body and are certainly a step in raising test scores.

CHAPTER 2

Understanding the Troubled Child

Teachers should always be on the lookout for students who have issues outside of the classroom that prevent them from performing at their highest level. A teacher could improve his or her understanding tremendously by focusing on the steps outlined in Chapter 1, yet a child may still not perform his or her best. Many issues prevent students from performing at their highest level. This does not mean that a teacher's expectations should waver toward any student. It means that although teachers recognize that "things" happen, they still should expect a child to do the best he or she can.

This chapter hinges on how to focus on students beyond academics. Teachers who take a personal interest in their students can typically get the most out of them academically, which is the ultimate benefit. The next part of the chapter focuses on the big picture of education, and it all starts with one child in one class. Once a teacher grasps this concept, he or she will be much more ready to address the things that may be holding back the class.

The three areas I find that affect a child's mood the most during a school year are bullying, divorce, and significant illness/death. I am focusing on mood first because when a child is not in the mood to learn, overall results are weakened. The areas I am referring to can cause an

A student to become a C student very quickly. It can take a lot of time to get a student back on track when he or she experiences one or more of these events. Here's the reason: academic principles build on one another. When a student experiences tremendous anxiety, he or she is not going to be as tuned into the teacher's lessons. When this anxiety occurs over a significant period of time, the child can be lost academically because the teacher will have moved on already in the curriculum. Some students do a better job of catching up academically than others, and that primarily is because of the teacher and the level the student started at before the event occurred. In other words, a strong student would have a much easier time recovering academically than a student with lower achievement.

The real key to facing these problems is to go one step beyond student engagement referred to in Chapter 1 into what I call *Personal Engagement*. A student who is truly engaged with his or her teacher is someone who can and will talk to the teacher during times of distress. Think of the child in kindergarten who raises his hand during a math lesson because he is excited for the teacher to know what he ate for dinner last night. Although I understand that a math class is not the time and place to talk about such topics, it is an example of a personal engagement.

Achieving personal engagement is easier with some students than with others. Here are three strategies I used and recommend to achieve personal engagement with students.

1. **Greet Students at the Door with a Smile**: I wanted to set a tone that my classroom was a warm and inviting place. On some days, you may not feel like smiling because of personal circumstances. On these days, you must completely fake it. It is imperative to start the day on a positive note with each student.

2. **Initiate Physical Contact with Students**: This is a tricky topic, so let me be clear about what I did. I gave a lot of side hugs, light pats on the shoulder, and high fives. I never had a student object to contact from me, but if that were the case, I would respect those wishes. I have always felt that physical contact brings people closer together. If you are to engage in physical contact, just be very careful to make sure your actions are interpreted correctly.

3. **Initiate Conversations about Nonschool-Related Matters**: I use this tactic, for example, during down times such as when a student is waiting to be called on a bus. Ask a child about a relative or his or her favorite sports team. There are certain students who really enjoy talking about elements of life outside of school. Once the connection is made, it is easier for these students to connect with you on in-school events. You should enjoy connecting with children not just as students, but also as people.

Being personally engaged with students is very important because they are more likely to confide in teachers when they have problems if they have a relationship beyond the classroom. Here are some problems that affect a child's mood in the classroom.

BULLYING AND TEASING

I'll introduce the topic of bullying in schools first because divorce and illness/death are out-of-school issues that are handled a bit differently. Personable engagement with a student who is a victim of bullying can pay big dividends quickly. I frequently tell my classes that if there is ever a bullying problem, they had better come tell me. I was a victim of some bullying in grade school, and I do not want other students to go through that same torment.

Teachers need to keep their fingers on the pulse of this issue of bullying because of all the emotional (not to mention academic) problems it causes. When students are personably engaged with their teachers, it makes the job of snuffing out the problem a lot easier. The students will come to you when there is a problem rather than the teachers trying to pry the problem out of the victims. The key is that the victim has to be more personally engaged with the teacher than scared of the bully. Even if the problem is not taken care of immediately, knowing that the teacher cares can place the victim in the correct frame of mind to do his or her best.

The prevention of bullying and teasing starts with the teacher's attitude. My frame of mind as a teacher is something like this: *I'm not going to let some bully ruin for a child everything I have worked to create.* Do not get me wrong. My primary concern is the victim of the bullying, but there is a selfish component as well. Because I know the feeling that bullies created inside of me, I am not going to let someone bully one of my students. I have worked too hard and too long for the child's progress to go to waste because my student is distracted by the bad behavior of others.

I fully recognize that some teachers are not confrontational. They may confuse bullying with "boys being boys." The problem will disappear with time, they think. The problem with this attitude is that teachers do not have the luxury of time. Material has to be taught and learned as quickly and efficiently as possible. Waiting for a problem to pass versus taking it head on will certainly cause a disruptive environment and lower test scores. If you are not a teacher who can handle a bullying problem, it is imperative that someone familiar with the situation or child do so. That could mean other faculty, a counselor, a principal, and/ or a parent. What is also important is that you know the laws on bullying in your jurisdiction, along with your responsibilities.

Although bullying and teasing are different problems, they are treated together in this chapter because they can make the victim feel scared. Bullying is never allowed in my classroom. I realize that sometimes friends playfully tease one another, so here is my philosophy: *When the person being teased isn't having a good time, the teasing better stop fast or I am going to get involved.*

DIVORCE

Of all the problems I have ever worked out, this one may be the most frustrating. I believe that many parents and teachers do not understand the toll this situation takes on a child. As educators, though, teachers have to deal with divorce and its effects on students and work their way through it. Unfortunately, when children in that circumstance take a standardized test, your state has no idea what is happening with those children on a personal basis. It is not as if teachers can check a "divorce box" so people can understand why a particular child did not do so well. In short, children are expected to perform as well as everyone else, even under this circumstance.

An Ohio State University research article found at http://research-news.osu.edu/archive/childdiv.htm quantified the problem in a startling manner. Yongmin Sun, coauthor of the study and an assistant professor at Ohio State, said,

The effects of divorce take two time paths. The damage in children's psychological well-being is already observable three years prior to divorce, but gets worse as the divorce approaches. Yet, as the event of divorce recedes, the detrimental effect becomes smaller, indicating a recovery in children's psychological well-being after the divorce. Test scores, however, continue to decline.

This study of almost ten thousand children started when they were in eighth grade. I do not believe it a stretch to imply, however, that divorce also affects younger children negatively as well.

Knowing this, the first thing a teacher must do is demonstrate strong leadership in the classroom. A similar approach is used as when a child has more chronic behavioral issues. The more occupied the child's mind is, the less problems at home can creep into his or her mind. This is one area where strong lesson planning really pays off. While lessons are going on, the child's mind can remain occupied with new and exciting material that will distract him or her while he or she is going through this unfortunate circumstance.

In my case, I was raised without a father. Although that is not the same as a divorce, my story appealed to many children because I had a personal connection to their circumstance. A 2010 study by the CDC (Centers for Disease Control and Prevention) said that 72.5 percent of African American children are born to unmarried mothers. I was amazed at how many fathers were no longer in the home. I never would have imagined, though, that the number was that high. Because of my story, I was able to encourage children even in other grades to keep going with their studies. I was also able to hold these students accountable because students weren't able to use their circumstance as a long-term excuse for failure with me. Sometimes, it can be helpful for students to be paired with staff who have gone through these types of circumstances for support. Another important approach is to place the student in contact with a school counselor because most staff members are not qualified on a professional level to handle these types of problems.

Again, the goal is to get and keep students on track as much as possible. Working out problems caused by a divorce takes a long time, and there are no short-term fixes, even if test time is looming. Improvement comes faster when the right adults are working on the problem.

DEATH

A lot of the concepts I submitted for a student going through a divorce can also be applied to a student going through a death in the family or of a friend. A teacher should want the right people working with the child in order to try to experience some normalcy in the classroom. Of course, if the teacher has experienced a significant death and he or she has a good rapport with the student, that is the best-case scenario. As with the case with divorce, the school counselor is also a valuable resource.

The most difficult situation I have experienced in dealing with death was with a second-grade student named Alexis. Her mother had died the year before (cancer, I believe), and she lived as an only child with her father. Alexis was one of the brightest students I have had the pleasure of working with in my teaching career. She was a clingy child, which is usually not acceptable with me. I made an exception from time to time in her case. Sometimes Alexis needed someone to cry to, and I was there for her. The important thing was that I was able to keep her on track academically as she was going through this difficult period in life.

SIGNS TO LOOK FOR IN THIS TYPE OF TROUBLED CHILD

I will reiterate that bullying/teasing, divorce, and death can ruin the best-laid lesson plans by any teacher. When teachers expect students to perform well without giving the extra time needed to deal thoroughly with these important issues, they have little idea of how the mind works.

More times than not, a child's inability to cope with problems will show up most clearly in his or her test scores.

There are times when teachers believe that parents should have all the answers to whatever is troubling their children and causing them to underperform. The reality is that some parents look at teachers and think the same thing. In the case of bullying and teasing, some parents may believe that *teachers see it all the time, so they know what to do*. This perception could be true even if their children are the ones perpetrating the harm. Teachers cannot simply take for granted that parents know what to do when their children are coping with big problems. Some parents are better than others. The weaker parents need the help of the teacher the most. In the case of divorce and death, the parent is often struggling as well, depending on the circumstances. Although parents have to be held responsible for their responsibilities, achieving the goal of a child "doing his or her best" is a community effort.

The signs to look for in this type of troubled child can be vast. The better relationship the child has with the teacher before the significant event (bullying, divorce, or death), the more likely the child will be to come address it with the teacher, which can make things much easier. Not all children fit this mold, however. Some children will act out when given instructions. The acting out can be frenzied, as when a child turns over a desk, or it can be complying with teacher requests but merely going through the motions. These children can be difficult to spot because of the time demands of the other children in class. The key is relationships, and that happens through personal engagement!

I realize the things I am discussing were probably not taught in college or discussed at the latest faculty meeting, but they are the reality of the teaching position. Teachers are like coaches. When coaches do not plan for various scenarios their teams can face during a season, they are more likely to lose games. Teachers have to plan and prepare, or they will lose as well. Facts are facts. Many teachers simply do not make the grade. In the end, though, the teacher is not the one who suffers the most (unlike a coach who can lose a six- to seven-figure a year job and be publicly humiliated). The ones who suffer the most are the students. School is hard, and depending on a child's overall cognitive level, he or she can be doomed when teachers overlook or fail to address problems.

ANOTHER POTENTIAL FACTOR FOR THE TROUBLED CHILD

Sooner or later, most children will be troubled. I don't have an actual percentage of the number of students who will experience these issues, but from my experience as a classroom teacher, I saw troubled children firsthand every year. Their troubles may arise for the reasons I've given or for another reason equally important.

Here is a personal story that I hope drives home the point. I was once a troubled teacher, and I remember quite well when the trouble started and why.

It started in a faculty meeting. My principal was highly upset because of the previous year's test scores (as best I remember). Anyway, the anger boiled over to the point where this person used curse words in front of the staff. As a man, I did not really care, but there were primarily women in the room. I could not believe his insensitivity and his lack of professionalism. Any principal should be able to make strong points without pushing language to that level.

Granted, I could have approached my principal and talked about it, but I took another route. Basically, I shut the person out. For about three months or so, I could not tell you about one conversation we had or one issue we talked about. I was professional, in general, but that is as far as it went. The unfortunate thing was that this principal was a really intelligent person. I probably could have learned a lot more than I did from him, but I was not willing to listen. Eventually, we had a conversation and hashed things out, but a lot of time was wasted between that point and the initial incident.

If my principal and I had had a better relationship, one of us would have probably approached the other, and the problem could have been resolved much more quickly. Since that wasn't the case, we had to make do. Making do isn't enough for children.

The troubles I listed above focused on events that could trouble a child. Another troubling factor often centers on grudges or misunderstandings. If a child doesn't like the teacher (whether the dislike is justified or not), he or she is going to be less likely to want to learn anything from that person for nine months. That does not mean that a teacher should bow down to a child's whim. It does mean, however, that problems have to be dealt with quickly or consequences will happen, regardless of intent.

One mistake I think teachers make is that they are so caught up in day to day operations that the totality of what needs to get accomplished gets lost. Most teachers know children from previous years who never seemed to learn what was required or who had a hard time with the desire to do the work. Typically, these children are the most difficult to work with and take the most time. Because of this, occasionally they are shoved aside. Teachers often do not have any negative intent behind "shoving." Here are two common scenarios:

1. The basic mind-set of the teacher may be *the class is ready to move on from this unit, and I have to continue with the curriculum, or we will fall behind the other classes, even if Jane doesn't get it."* There is a lot of truth behind this logic. If the class always waited for

Jane to "get it," little work could potentially be accomplished, which is disastrous for all students in the class. The problem lies within the mentality. The teacher should have known that Jane was going to struggle before the unit began and prepared accordingly. If the teacher waits until the test results come back, the damage has already been done.

2. Another possible thought process is *to let sleeping dogs lie.* In this case, a teacher may suspect that Jane doesn't fully comprehend the material but doesn't take extra steps because of the child's attitude. In other words, as long as the child stays quiet, all is well. Again, there is some logic in this. The teacher may know that the child's parental situation is not good or give some other reason that justifies the "shoving." The answer to this dilemma also starts before the unit should ever begin. If a teacher knows a child's attitude could potentially interfere with the overall learning, he or she must address it.

The totality of the situation is a lot different. Units in most subject areas build on one another. If students do not understand a unit and are forced to move on, the odds of catching up are not high. Obviously, when one unit is compromised, the odds of the next unit not being understood completely are significantly higher. The extreme example of this issue would be the high school student who gets a diploma but doesn't even know how to read.

The concept of "shoving" gets expanded even more based on the number of classrooms in a school. Almost all teachers have inadequately performing students who do not understand the material well enough to justify moving forward. When test time comes around, these students are not in a position to perform very well. They are the collateral damage of any school. Statistically speaking, if the "shoving" happened only to one child, I doubt anyone would ever know (except possibly the parents). But it is not a stretch to believe that "shoving" happens a lot. Again, the test scores never lie.

What is worse than the "shoving" is that many of the struggling students have a clue about what is going on. They know they are not performing well. Therefore, these students typically act out in some way—by becoming the class clown, the bully, or the one who always looks out of the window, etc. As the child's advances in his or her school career, each one will be eventually known as "The Troubled Child." It is almost a self-fulfilling prophesy.

CHAPTER 3
All Learning Starts with Motivation

One misconception that I have seen from teachers through observations and discussions is that classroom management as was discussed in chapter one leads directly to learning. Classroom management is vital. In saying that though, a teacher can have a well behaved class without a lot of learning going on. Just because little Johnny is not throwing a chair in class or little Sally is no longer talking out of turn doesn't mean much if they (and all of the other students) do not leave your classroom smarter than when they walked in.

True learning starts when students are motivated. Generally speaking, I would rather have a motivated child who is a little behind grade level than an unmotivated child who is slightly ahead in their grade level. Over time, a motivated child will continue to work hard when the curriculum gets difficult. Consequently, that child will surpass others who may have a bit more academic talent but are less motivated. I would also trust a motivated child taking a standardized test more than someone less motivated. That's because on testing day, I know I am going to get a premium effort from the motivated child. It's less certain what kind of effort will be given from another child with less motivation.

Several years ago, I had a second-grade student named Tirzah in my class who was one of my bottom five readers as graded by the DRA (Developmental Reading Assessment). It took a collaborative effort of caring professionals but one key thing she was missing was motivation. What was amazing about Tirzah was that once she became motivated, she worked hard and left my classroom as one of my top five readers.

Not all children are motivated in the same way. It's important for teachers to study and execute the seven motivational tactics presented. These tactics have been used on the hardest children I have ever worked with to great success. The trick is figuring out which tactic will work the best. This is one of the reasons why building meaningful teacher/student relationships is critical. Here are my seven motivational tools.

1. MOTIVATE THROUGH ENCOURAGEMENT (INDIVIDUALLY, AS A CLASS, THROUGH FOCUSED ENCOURAGEMENT, EYE CONTACT, ENCOURAGEMENT THROUGH PROOF)

This form of motivation is something most teachers do in varying degrees. I think if I polled any given school, 9.9 out of 10 teachers would say that they encourage students. Therefore, we will expand this topic in order to demonstrate how and why encouraging students was successful in the classes I taught and with my children at home.

Encouragement should occur daily on an individual basis but also as a whole class. The rule of thumb for me as a teacher was *no matter how much I encouraged others; there was always room for more.* Small encouragement lessons start right from the beginning of the year for a whole class. The reason I liked to start encouraging the whole class first (versus individuals) is that it is time efficient. Also, the teacher gets to size up the entire class at the same time. Teachers can take mental notes as to who is responding positively and which students may need a different tactic. It sets the tone early in the year. What teachers will find is that it is difficult for students to be negative for a long stretch of time in front of strong encouragers.

Here's an example of a whole class encouragement talk before a lesson begins:

Boys and girls, you are going to be so happy you came to school today. I heard some outstanding reading and class participation yesterday, and I'm positive I'm going to hear more today. There were three words we struggled with while reading as a class (Teacher writes the words on the board). *We may miss ten other words today, but we are conquering these three words. You know you can do it. I know you can do it. I want to see who the fastest children are to open their books to page twenty-five, starting…now!*

At this point, the lesson begins. What is important for the teacher is an upbeat delivery. Teachers should portray a positive aura right from the start of a lesson. As far as taking up valuable class time, the above monologue should take under a minute. It is not exactly practical to encourage for half an hour and teach for only twenty minutes!

Teachers must also observe whether any of the children deemed "behavior problems" made eye contact during the quick monologue. Instead of attacking the student for not paying attention, I might approach the student privately and assess whether he or she knows the three problematic words on the board. If the student knows any of them, I am going to give a quick, encouraging comment. Even if the student misses all three words and I am privately thinking, Oh goodness, are you kidding me? I will still go over the words again. The overall goal is for the student to learn the words on the board. The student cannot escape my attention until I can say something positive. On a short-term basis, what I am talking about may seem trivial. On a big picture basis, however, I need all students to have a favorable attitude toward learning and an interest in what I am trying to accomplish. The material obviously gets harder, and students need to know I will be there when those times occur.

The key to the example of encouragement above is that it has to be meaningful. Sometimes, human nature sets in. A teacher, for example, who does not like the student he or she is working with has to set those emotions aside. Also, if the student hasn't shown the ability to perform very well academically, staying positive can be especially difficult. Encouraging students—even when a particular student has given the teacher twenty reasons not to be encouraging—is still the best way to help the student do his or her best.

An area where I have seen teachers make a mistake while encouraging students involves solid eye contact. A high-school teacher taught me that when a person looks, he or she listens twice, once with his or her ears and once with his or her eyes. I have found that there is a lot of truth in that statement. The eye-to-eye contact helps a student see a teacher's conviction when the encouragement is given.

Teachers should keep in mind that cultures have different beliefs in terms of eye contact. In certain Asian, African, and Latin American cultures, extended eye contact may be considered rude. All cultures should be respected. Therefore, if I know a certain culture does not encourage eye contact, I do not force it. On the other hand, for cultures that encourage eye contact, I strongly encourage it. "Eye Contact: What Does it Communicate in Various Cultures?" is an informative article found on the Bright Hub Education website. It provides some insights into various cultures and their beliefs concerning eye contact. (You can find the article at http://www.brighthubeducation.com/social-studies-help/9626-learning-about-eye-contact-in-other-cultures/)

The final tactic I enjoy using to motivate children is through "proof." This method is powerful when the whole class engages in it and even more powerful when done on an individual level. Encouraging through proof may look something like this:

Hey, class, guess what? I have your spelling tests in my hand. I told you that if you worked hard, our class would get a B average. Well, you all must have worked hard because that is exactly what happened. Make sure you learn the lesson, though, boys and girls. When you work toward a goal and put the time in, you are a winner in my eyes. I want you to go home, get these tests signed, and tell mom and dad how proud I am to be your teacher.

When teachers motivate their classes through proof, the students feel they can accomplish anything. It is a great setup for future tests and assessments. Although ability ultimately determines the success of students, belief is a major part of the battle.

Motivating through proof is one of the surest ways I could turn around a child who had a "behavior problem." I liked to find something the child did well, guide the child in such a way to make him or her better, and capitalize on it through sheer motivation. That would mean, for example, that if a child was a decent math student, I could motivate by saying something like this: *You are so talented, child! Let's take that math attitude and use it during writing class. I believe in what you are doing, and I'm proud of you!* By the time writing class started, that child, more times than not, brought a good attitude to class. Most teachers I have worked with could take children and build on their skills. The trick was to have the child in the correct state of mind so the teacher could maximize potential.

2. MOTIVATE THROUGH SIGNS

Classroom walls are not being fully utilized when they hold only a letter chart, hundred chart, and some student work. The walls can be a place to practice reading and find encouragement when teachers place motivational signs all around the room Teachers should make sure they place their favorite signs close to the seat of the "challenging child." One of my favorite signs to hang is *Success is a Choice*. These types of signs serve the visual learners well.

Teachers should change their signs every couple of weeks so that children do not become immune to the messages in the signs (similar to the hundred chart). Visual learners need constant stimulation for this tactic to work. Anytime a sign is changed, it must be talked about with the students in order to achieve the maximum effect. For ideas on signs, simply type "motivational signs for children" into a web search engine. Teachers will find more than they need.

3. MOTIVATE THROUGH COMPETITION

Some teachers may not like the idea of learning through competition, but for some students, it does work well. I am a competitive person, and in the real world, people compete daily. In my mind, there is nothing wrong with introducing the concept to youngsters.

The concept of winning and losing is highly motivational. There is a risk that a troubled child will not react well when losing a competition, but the reverse could be true as well. It strictly depends on the child. Sometimes, teachers have to take chances with children. Students should not be confused with computers. They do not always have predictable outcomes.

One reason I motivate students with the competition theme in the classroom dates back to when I was in the third grade. Ms. Bauman was my teacher, and I remember only two things from the entire year. The first memory is that she was one of the nicest educators I have had at any grade. The second memory is board races during math class. She would let us have some fun with these races if we behaved and did a good job during class. I will guarantee you that despite my poor memory of the grade, I would never have misbehaved in her class because I loved competing against my friends. Her strategy also made me pretty quick at math.

The only caution I give to teachers is that they shouldn't set up a child to fail. With any competition, some children win while others do not. Therefore, it is important for teachers to change any competitive educational games so that the same children are not always losing. For example, I wouldn't have students playing math board races every week. Over time, the same children typically win. Also, playing educational games in groups can help offset the same children losing.

I loved letting the children compete at nearly anything inside or outside the classroom. The key was the motivation after the event. There was nothing like taking a difficult student aside and praising the effort for competing. It let the child know I was paying attention, and it made the student work that much harder in order to garner additional praise. It is a noble feat for children to learn for the love of learning, but that doesn't always work. Trying a different tactic is sometimes necessary.

4. MOTIVATE THROUGH ACCOUNTABILITY

Being accountable in the classroom means a teacher gives an assignment, and the student accomplishes it in a timely manner. If the student struggles, it is his or her responsibility to ask for help. Accountability works both ways. Teachers should anticipate who will need help before the assignment begins and make the necessary arrangements. Being prepared in this way may sound easy on the surface, but it is not. Teachers have too many students, and some students simply will not ask for help. Those are the ones who are likely to fall through the cracks. So how does a teacher hold a child accountable? The answer lies within the attitude of the teacher.

Suppose, for example, that a teacher has a child who does not turn in some homework. Most teachers would probably say something like *Well, make sure you turn in your homework tomorrow.* Children who typically have their homework and simply make a mistake shouldn't need much more motivation. For other children forgetting homework is more of a problem. Typically, these same students also have the lower scores in the class.

Teachers need to hold these students more accountable, which can be done in a variety of ways. If I have a good relationship with the student, the best tactic for me has been showing displeasure when the child is not doing the things that are his or her responsibility (homework, in this case). This tactic may sound simplistic on the surface, but there is more to it. I was typically a very happy teacher. Therefore, when I showed displeasure, it was almost shocking to a child. The other thing I did was choose my words carefully. I may have said something like *You know you are smart enough to do your homework. You are letting me down, and you are letting yourself down. Take care of the problem.* Did you happen to catch the psychology? If not, read the mock answer one more time.

You know you are smart enough to do your homework states one thing. It also implies another idea. The first message is that the child is smart—an underlying confidence booster that is a strong form of motivation. The implication, however, is that if a student does not do his or her homework, your teacher does not believe that he or she is smart. Students who have a good relationship with their teachers do not want the teacher to think of them as unintelligent. Please be careful with this concept, though. I have seen teachers try to use psychology before, and it comes off as sarcasm, which is not good. It diminishes the overall quality of the teacher/student relationship. Students take teachers who act in a professional manner more seriously than those who are sarcastic.

Another effective motivator through accountability is the use of consequences. One complaint I have heard from teachers is the lack of effective ways to apply consequences. There is some truth to this concern. But consequences should be intended only to teach—not to punish. Therefore, I could argue that any consequence is effective when a student learns his or her lesson. Sometimes, though, a student has to be taught a lesson multiple times before it completely sinks in. That can be frustrating for teachers to accept, but again, teachers are not working with computers. Going back to the homework example, it is a common practice at my son's school to take away recess and have students walk around the recess perimeter. Are there some children who have to walk the perimeter a few times for the lesson to set in? Sure! But most students want to play, and it's not fun to walk while their buddies are playing. Sooner or later, the student will get the message.

Once this happens, I would *motivate with encouragement.* For example I would say, *I am so proud you are going to be able to play with your buddies today at recess. When you are playing with your buddies, remember the feeling. If you do not turn in the homework tomorrow, you will be walking again, and we would not want that!*

5. MOTIVATE THROUGH REWARDS

Students are like most adults I know. They like to be rewarded for hard work. One problem I have seen time and time again is that teachers do not stop to smell the roses when things go as planned. It is almost as if they take it for granted if the class receives a B average on the assessment after studying a difficult unit. The truth is that school can be very hard, and it is all right to reward students when things go well.

Children who can have discipline problems enjoy rewards as well, which should be used to a teacher's advantage. The easiest reward a teacher might give is a sticker. I like stars and cute pictures, but I am partial to the ones with motivational messages such as "great job" or "you did it." I also like it when children compare their stickers because they might work harder next time to get their buddies' sticker messages.

Children who were more difficult to educate would not only receive a sticker, but would also get a pat on the back or some type of message from me. The key is that I want the student to buy into what I am doing in order to limit future discipline problems. The most successful teachers I have worked with typically look ahead and see how a given moment can have a positive impact on future ones. But here is one cautionary note. Over time, stickers tend to be less motivating, so teachers who use this type of motivation have to be a bit creative. My solution is to order from the Oriental Trading company. It has little knickknacks at a reasonable cost. Children like getting these rewards from me simply because they are a little different.

Teachers should also remember to choose their reward battles. I was not a teacher who rewarded every little thing. That way, when I did pull down my rewards bucket from the top shelf, students knew they had done something that I thought deserved recognition.

Teachers have to use discretion, but one thing I did not reward was good behavior. My rewards were academically based. I wanted students learning in my classroom. If a child, for example, behaved well but didn't learn much, I would consider that a wasted day. Let me put this in another way: *Good behavior is a by-product of learning.* In other words, when children are busy learning, they are not misbehaving. I do not recall in my teaching career watching a student misbehave and learn at the same time.

One fun reward a teacher can try giving a misbehaving child is the "one grade up" reward, which means that if a student flunked a test, he or she could get a reward if on the next test he or she scored one grade up. Children who earned an A can get a reward if they earn another A. I have seen teachers give rewards for situations such as the top ten grades or for students who get a B on a given assessment. One difficulty with those conditions is that a teacher may have a child who is not capable of fulfilling the reward conditions at that time. Often the child feels alienated if everyone else gets a reward. That is why I like one grade up. All the children still compete. But their main competition is themselves (specifically their last grade) versus other students. I acknowledge that a child could still fail with my reward system. What I am claiming is that the child has a much higher chance of success. As the old saying goes, "Success breeds success." Therefore, if I can help a child know what it is like to earn the reward once, it is probable that I can continue to motivate the child to continue working hard to do his or her best.

6. MOTIVATE THROUGH PRIDE

I believe that pride is natural. The development of pride though can be nurtured, and that is where teachers can really make a difference. Therefore, I am going to address the pride angle on two fronts. The first angle is what I did with students who have shown characteristics of pride. The second angle will deal with students who had minimal to zero pride in themselves. With either type of student, teachers should remember this: *Students cannot give their best effort when they do not take pride in themselves and in their work.* Please remember that pride does not necessarily relate to the child's academic ability. In theory, a child can take pride in his or her work and still fail the class.

A child who takes pride in his or her work will do his or her best to listen to the teacher, complete the homework, and ask questions when needed. Some teachers may disagree with the last point of asking questions. They would argue that some children are too full of pride or maybe too shy to ask questions. The truth is those teachers are confusing pride with shame. Some students may not want to ask a question because they fear the reaction of other students, and/or the teacher may be negative. It is hard for some people to admit when they need help. Even many adults possess this trait. It is imperative that students understand the difference. Those who do will raise their hands in class much more often.

Students who show characteristics of pride are easier to work with versus other students who have yet to understand the concept. It doesn't matter how much of a behavior problem a child can be. If the student shows some pride, a teacher should note it and use the information when needed.

When I saw a child misbehaving who had pride, I could always walk up to the student and use a variety of quick responses. One example would be, *Get to work and show me you can do better.* That response is quick and easy, and it worked often. There were times I went a little deeper to get my point across. I may whisper in a child's ear, *You are making yourself look bad. Straighten up, and get back to work before someone else notices.* When I would say something like that, there would be more inflection in my tone. Children knew that I meant business.

Children who have not shown pride in themselves have to be taught. Have you ever heard a child say, *I don't care* after being given a direction or shown a test result? Sometimes, that phrase is used as a defense mechanism. The child is saying in other words, *I do not want the teacher to know how I really feel.* Other times, though, the child is serious. He or she does not really care at that moment. That is why I want teachers to understand that *pride starts with caring.* When students show they care (even a little bit) about themselves or their work, a teacher, at that point, has a foundation to build on.

Each assignment students complete is a reflection of themselves, their school, and their family. Students who have not shown a lot of pride in themselves need to start with this foundation. It is important for students to attach themselves to a person to whom they could be held accountable. One reason the teacher/student relationship is so important is that the person I am talking about is directly in the child's line of sight. A teacher can always say to a student that his or her mother really wants the student to do well so the child should try his or her best. Don't get me wrong, moms (and dads) are really important. But mom and dad are not staring at the child for thirty hours a week. If the teacher can be a person the child cares about, the seeds of pride can be planted within the student.

Over time, teachers should want students to transition from doing assignments because they care about their teachers to doing assignments because they care about themselves and the work. But for some students, that is too much of a jump to make. The goal for the teacher is to set the "pride foundation" and build on it. On a personal level, I will tell you that this approach takes a lot of time and work, but once the foundation has been set, behavior problems nearly disappear, and student learning improves significantly.

7. MOTIVATE THROUGH NOTES

This may be one of the oldest tricks I know. I actually got the idea from moms and dads who place notes in their children's lunch boxes. It was really neat to watch a child pull out a note from a loved one. The child's face would brighten, and the note seemed to make the child happy.

There are many ways to use notes as motivational tools. For example, a teacher could write inspiring words on a chalkboard for students to see when they walk into a room. One example may be *Hey, Kayla and Dominique, Love the math work yesterday. Keep it up!* This approach is simple and time effective. Obviously, though, if a teacher uses the board, he or she must use it consistently so a kind comment can appear for all students. Failure to do so could make a child feel alienated. A child who feels alienated obviously cannot do his or her best, which defeats the entire purpose.

Another way to pull off this idea is through Post-it Notes. Give a quick message to a few children but not to everyone at the same time. You want to make the child receiving the note feel special. There is not anything wrong with targeting children who present occasional behavioral challenges, but a teacher still has to be careful not to alienate other students. Therefore, if a teacher is going to use this idea, he or she should use it with consistency.

Being a good motivator is an important skill for a teacher. It gives an educator a foundation for building on students' potential. The ability to motivate also significantly cuts behavior problems. Children will come into the classroom excited and ready to learn. Teachers can become better motivators by practicing various ideas I have presented, seeing what the students respond to the best, and assessing which ideas fit into their personality and teaching style.

Finally, teachers should remember that the motivational messages presented are not just for students. Over the course of the school year, teachers have to find ways to keep themselves motivated to perform at their optimal level. Jeanne Flowers, a former principal and one of the editors of this book, recommended a "motivational box." The box should contain encouraging notes for the teacher to read often to the class during the year. Although I did not do this, it is an excellent idea and one I highly recommend.

Over time, teachers who are not motivated eventually find themselves in a rut. Being in a rut is horrible for many reasons. Teachers in a rut may have trouble with children who have behavior problems because they lack creative ideas to solve problems those children can create. Nine months is a long time to teach the same group of children. Therefore, teachers should make sure to motivate one another and seek out other forms of motivation (books, videos, etc). It is amazing to watch a motivated teacher work and see the eyes of the students who are taking in every word.

CHAPTER 4

The Expectation Attitude

I am certain that teachers who have taught for more than a day realize that the art of teaching goes far beyond the books, notebooks, paper, and pencils. This chapter is going to delve into directing young minds as soon as they enter the classroom because the children are motivated and mentally ready to take their education to the next level.

One thing I discovered during my years of teaching was that most teachers believed they had high expectations of students. The problem was that I believe the term high expectations is overused and under defined. What having high expectations from one teacher may be completely different than another teacher. When I fully implemented the expectation attitude, teaching became the most fun for me. It was at this level that students were fully ready to learn. Teachers should recognize this point and be able to proceed with great confidence.

There are three parts to the expectation attitude. The first part is what the classroom teacher expects from the students. The second part is what the teachers should expect from themselves. The third part focuses on what the students should expect from themselves. Teachers need to understand that the third part is the ultimate goal.

Some astute teachers reading this may believe there should be a fourth goal. It would read *what students should expect from the teacher*. If a teacher is not giving his or her best effort, he or she needs to find a new profession. This job is far too important for students to expect anything less than the maximum effort from their teachers on a daily basis.

PART 1 OF THE EXPECTATION ATTITUDE (TEACHER EXPECTATIONS OF STUDENTS)

My goal is for students to come into the classroom and do their best. Young students need to realize that when they do their best, they maximize their potential. I taught students that maximizing potential is nothing less than a sign of greatness. I wanted all of my students to be great. If a student fell short of this expectation, I wanted to know why and to address the problem immediately.

Teachers should not fear expecting greatness from students as long as they have fully built the educational foundation described in the first three chapters. I have seen many teachers settle for mediocrity from students for a variety of reasons. When a teacher demands anything less than the best a student has to offer, one thing is for sure—that teacher will certainly get it.

One reason I think teachers expect less than greatness from their students is that they may find the goal unattainable or too time-consuming. It is easier for teachers to simply prepare lessons, help whomever they can, give an assessment, and write down the grade. Most of the time the same students get the A's, and the same students get the D's and F's. Great teachers know there is more to the equation.

A second reason some teachers accept mediocrity is that certain students react negatively when challenged, which can lead to behavior problems. Although it is easier to leave these students alone, teachers need to push through that barrier. I have had a number of students who entered my classroom not used to a demanding style of teaching. Changing their expectations certainly took time, but I was amazed by how many of these students responded to my challenges and surpassed my expectations.

Another reason some teachers accept mediocrity is that expecting greatness from students involves real work. For example, let's suppose teacher A is educating a third-grade math class. What most people come to understand quickly is that the third-grade class is not full of third graders. In fact, there will be three to four students who could learn in a fourth-grade classroom today, four to five students who are several months ahead, even if they should not go into a fourth-grade classroom, eight to ten students who are learning material that is appropriate, and three to four students who belong in a second-grade classroom. The numbers may be slightly off for some classrooms during a given year, but they represent the average I have found during my years of teaching. If a teacher is not determined and does not have a plan to "reach" each child, then the odds are that the teacher will not. Part of this reaching process involves creating multiple lesson plans.

When students understand that demanding more from themselves creates more academic success, there is a snowball effect. Don't get me wrong—there are going to be many challenges and problems along the way, but teachers who have higher expectations and know how to get the most out of children typically have higher scoring students than their peers.

Changing the expectation attitude starts with attacking the breakdown of the student ratios described above. For example, one thing I like to do is focus on my inadequately performing students and set a goal that they will get at least a letter grade higher than they normally achieve on assessments. One of my principals actually charted the students with low achievement in every grade. He had chart paper with the names of all these students taped up on his walls and updated the information as the school year went along. Teachers should not implement this same plan because student grades are private, but they can assess at-risk students, set up small groups of struggling students from the beginning of a unit, and reinforce information taught in class every day until the test at the end of the unit. It is vital for a teacher to expect a student to do his or her best. But if there is not a written plan to reach the goal, the student is much more likely to perform below expectations.

Concerning the higher-level students: teachers should not feel good about their work unless they know the students actually learned something. In other words, if a student could have received an A on the test before the material was taught, then the student did not learn anything, and valuable time was wasted. Teachers need to expect more from higher-level students. A pretest given before a unit is introduced will allow a teacher to understand who needs the current material and who should be given more challenging work. From there, higher-level students can be given extension assignments, or they can advance to a more challenging unit. I have seen many situations in which higher-level students become unpaid teaching assistants for students with low achievement. Although it could be argued that the attitude is noble, all children should be in school learning, meeting expectations, and being pushed to higher levels.

PART 2 OF THE EXPECTATION ATTITUDE (WHAT TEACHERS SHOULD EXPECT FROM THEMSELVES)

Teachers also have to have an expectation of themselves. The expectation should be that they will be the best teachers, and they will work as hard as it takes. Educators must expect the most from themselves. They must put the time in, target the problem students, and set up action plans that would be the envy of other teachers. The results for teachers who set high goals for themselves are predictable: they get more out of their students and have fewer behavior problems.

Every teacher should have the goal of finding someone who is a better teacher (at his or her school or another) and become that teacher's best friend (figuratively speaking). The goal, of course, is to get to know what makes that particular teacher so good. What qualities does this teacher possess? What are his or her discipline strategies? How does he or she approach struggling students? Which professional development training programs has he or she attended? What do his or her time-management skills look like? The most important question for a mentor may be *which steps will he or she take to become an even better teacher?* When a teacher knows the answer to these types of questions, he or she can take a giant step in becoming one of the best.

Great teachers have to take their careers as seriously as great athletes, scientists, or surgeons do. Most people, for example, would think of Kobe Bryant as being one of the greatest basketball players in the world today. What is interesting, though, is that I have listened to many of his teammates. To a man, they have all said that he is the hardest working player on the team. One may think that once you are among the best, it is time to relax. But it is the drive to become one of the best that prevents a person from relaxing.

Great teachers do not look at problematic children as excuses. Rather, they view them as challenges similar to a Rubik's cube. In other words, there is a solution. Finding it may take a lot of patience along with some twists and turns. Eventually though, these teachers expect that the problems will be solved.

PART 3 OF THE EXPECTATION ATTITUDE (WHAT STUDENTS SHOULD EXPECT FROM THEMSELVES)

One thing that teachers will find is that the expectation attitude is contagious. Therefore, when teachers are open about what they expect from the class, there will typically be a couple of student leaders who will take the cue. As I mentioned before, there is a snowball effect. When children who typically misbehave see and feel the weight of the expectations, they typically fall into line over time. There is a positive vibe in the air that is unmistakable. Ask principals who have observed all of their classrooms—they know exactly where high expectations prevail and where they do not.

In *Tantrums, Troubles, and Treasures*, I told a story about a boy I called Ryan. Ryan was a second grader with severe behavior problems. He had been suspended from school based on behaviors such as cursing out teachers, turning over desks in the middle of lessons, and fighting. I had a tremendous academic class that year and could have ignored the situation easily. During faculty meetings, his teacher complained over and over. The teacher's complaints got to the point of being sickening because there was no way this child was going to learn anything, and his antics were keeping his classmates from learning.

I volunteered to take the child when the teacher needed a breather—he was in my room the next day. At first, I expected some type of fight from him, which I was completely ready to deal with. Instead, nothing happened, even when he asked me about going back to his classroom and I told him, "no." I found his behavior interesting because children typically do not like to be told no. The other thing I noticed about the child was that he was well groomed, which told me someone was taking care of him at home and that his mother or father could potentially be used as a resource. Even though I was returning him to his classroom the next day, I had the feeling that he was someone I could work with.

Over the next couple of weeks, more trouble (and suspensions) occurred in Ryan's other classroom. He came to my room a handful of times, and, again, nothing happened in terms of poor behavior. One of the more memorable points of this ordeal happened when I was teaching a whole group reading lesson. I remember asking the class a question, and Ryan raised his hand. I called on him, and he got the right answer. Now I had a different situation on my hands. I not only had a child behaving, but he was listening and learning. I had another child absent from school that day, so I raised my voice a bit and told Ryan, "Only troublemakers sit in the back of my room. Real students sit in desks. Get out of that chair, sit at this desk, and be a real student." Shortly after that, Ryan made a permanent classroom switch. Weeks later, I met his mother, and I was right about the grooming observation. His mother was a terrific lady who did a great job in catching up her child academically. She even volunteered on certain days to sit with her son during reading class.

Although I take full responsibility for setting the tone in my class, I have to give a lot of credit to the other students concerning the development of Ryan. I had already had talks with my students about wanting to be the best class in the school. They set high expectations of themselves to listen and do their best. By the time Ryan entered my classroom, we were in high gear. An expression I heard as a teacher was that one bad apple could ruin the whole cart. That type of thinking seemed to open the door for excuses for a class not performing as well as it could. I had a different approach to that old saying: *If one bad apple got in the way of my train, that apple wasn't going to last long.*

Students owe it to themselves to see how well they can do in the classroom. Although teachers should have high expectations, there is a point where students should take on the weight and responsibilities of these expectations, which can easily start as early as kindergarten and develop over the course of time.

One question I enjoyed asking students was, why are you here? This simple question, if asked in the right spirit, can really propel students to having higher expectations of themselves. If the question is asked by a respected teacher who has high expectations, it can really be effective. Many students answer, "To learn." That response is a great starting point, but pushing students on this question can really pay dividends over time.

Using follow-up questions was a favorite method of mine. For example, I might ask questions such as, Learn what? or Why do you think you should learn that? This tactic places students in the proper mind-set. What it also does is give the teacher ammunition in the event that the student misbehaves in the future. Even if a student has high expectations of himself or herself, that doesn't mean the student will not occasionally regress. It is the teacher's job to get the student on track as quickly as possible and allow the student to continue his or her educational journey.

CHAPTER 5

Circling the Educational Wagons

Teachers will realize over time that children can still fall through the cracks, even if they are doing their best. There is a reason for this: education is a numbers game, and the numbers are not on the side of the teacher. When I refer to the numbers game, I am specifically talking about the student to teacher ratio. This chapter will present an aggressive way to turn the numbers game back into the favor of the people who need it most.

The status quo of teachers closing their doors and working with their students alone has not produced the numeric results most schools want to achieve. Teachers also must understand that the administrations they work with can only do so much to help. I have seen principals and counselors roll up their sleeves and work in classrooms, but even they could not be everywhere at once. Principals can only afford to hire a set number of teachers and instructional assistants. Schools have tight budgets, and the principals I worked with stretched those budgets as much as possible.

I find it interesting that although budgets are getting tighter, demands on teachers are growing. For example, many concepts that used to be introduced in first grade are now introduced in kindergarten. This shift places added pressure on teachers to make sure these concepts are being taught. Obviously, if there is any type of failure, the effects can be felt by students as time goes on and as more difficult concepts are introduced. It would be nice if the department of education gave more time for teachers to go deeper into subjects. The reality is that the pressure seems to mount as the years go on, and I do not look for that to change.

Schools would have a powerful tool if they could hold parents accountable for the completion of homework and low test scores, but the truth is that schools cannot count on parents in this respect. I remember during my teaching days that educators would often express concern about the lack of parent support during faculty meetings. Although I understood and agreed with their point, it was an exercise in futility.

I have watched many teachers fall to the numbers game—not because of lack of dedication or lack of experience. Rather, it was because teachers cannot be everywhere at once. They don't have the capacity to juggle one child misbehaving with another student who is doodling and another child who simply needs extra time and help to understand the material. While these things are going on, the majority of the class is waiting for its next assignment.

In order to combat the numbers game problem, teachers have to have a completely different mind-set. For the trends to turn, teachers have to take ownership of test scores similar to the way many would if they were dealing with their own children. In order to take control, teachers must recognize and confront the numbers game. Teachers have to recognize that they need additional help. This means they have to recruit volunteers from outside areas if there are not enough parents to fill the void. Teachers need a clear idea of the number of volunteers needed, the times they are needed, the students who will be using them, and the clear purpose of the volunteers' time. An effective plan would look something like this:

Teacher Bob (who teaches fourth grade) needs four hours of volunteer time per week. He needs two hours to be devoted to reading. Student Susie and student Earl need the most help because they are reading on a mid-third-grade level. One hour needs to be devoted to math. Students Juan and Julian need additional help with their knowledge of fractions. One hour can be spent on Simon and Paul, who have shown an extraordinary writing talent and could be paired with Kenton (in fifth grade) who has struggled with the concept of "how-to" essays.

Before attempting to recruit volunteers, teachers must understand there much is involved for the goal to work.

1. Volunteers have to be trained. State, local, district, and religious guidelines have to be followed. Privacy issues must be addressed. Some volunteers tend to talk, especially to friends who are also volunteering. A clear expectation must be established that students' privacy will be maintained.

2. Teachers must be willing to communicate with a student's previous teachers to pinpoint when the student started to struggle academically. If the student is a year or more behind his peers, the previous teacher may be able to help with material that would benefit the child. A teacher cannot just throw some supplemental work at a volunteer and expect to wash his or her hands of the child. Also, if the student transferred from another school, a teacher should not hesitate to call the prior school and create a game plan with the previous teacher. From there, the volunteer/teacher must establish a solid plan to catch the student up with his or her peers. When I worked with my own children, I was

amazed by how quickly they could absorb information when assignments were laser focused and distractions were limited. The volunteer, at that point, must be comfortable with implementing the game plan and have the material ready to do the moment the student walks in the door.

3.   Volunteers must be made to feel part of the school community. They need to feel an intrinsic value. When their work is not acknowledged, they tend not to come back.

4.   Volunteers should be at school only to improve student success. They should never be making copies, grading papers, creating bulletin boards, or performing menial tasks. Their sole purpose (with the teacher as the guide) is to help a student who wants to succeed and needs an extra pair of hands to ensure this happens.

5.   Volunteers should be matched to students on the basis of their strengths and personality. A student who misbehaves should not be thrown at a volunteer in order to give the teacher a break. On the other hand, volunteers who are good at working with students with behavior problems may be trusted (on a short leash) to work with that type of student. During my years as a teacher, I made the volunteer appear to be a privilege for the struggling student. For example, I may say to the student, "I want you to do well. But if you decide to give (Ms. Jones) any trouble, I will pair her up with another student, and you will never work with her again. Am I clear?" I will tell you that I never had to pair a volunteer with another student once "the talk" was given.

Maybe it was because the student really wanted a break from me. I do not mind being the bad guy for a while if it means that a student is working to do his or her best.

6. Teacher should not pair all volunteers with the lowest-performing children. Some should work with students who already know the material and need enrichment lessons to move further ahead.

7. Volunteers should be distributed as evenly as possible throughout the classrooms. The goal should be to help the entire student body. If one grade has eight consistent volunteers while another grade has only one, the effectiveness of the volunteer program is diminished. Organizers should start with the premise that volunteers are there for the good of the school, not for the teacher. From there, they must consider where volunteers should spend their time to be most effective.

8. Volunteers should be given the option of tasks versus time. Some people may not be able to give up an hour per week. These people may prefer to tackle a specific project. For example, a teacher may ask a volunteer to apply strategies that build quicker multiplication skills for three fourth graders. Once the fourth graders demonstrate they have mastered the task, the volunteer can be thanked and asked to help with another task at a later time. This strategy takes the pressure off people who do not want to lock up their time indefinitely.

Some schools really seem to have trouble attracting good volunteers. From what I have seen, one reason is that teachers tend to give up a bit too easily. Teachers do not like to be rejected, stood up, or not taken seriously in their request for help. It takes courage to ask people to volunteer. Teachers must have their students in mind and then ask this question: Is it worth being turned down a dozen times in order to gain four or five volunteers who would ultimately help struggling students, limit behavior problems, and raise test scores by several points?

I understand that some teachers will not want to do the work and get on board. They would rather shut their classroom doors and handle all of the educational issues alone. A good teacher, however, cannot let that attitude permeate the positive changes they are creating for the school. Changing and getting out of comfort zones are not easy things to do. Insanity is doing the same thing over and over and expecting a different result. Teachers who have students who could improve with a little extra help will eventually have some explaining to do when their peers show solid and undeniable results. With that said, here is a list of ways to grab the best volunteers teachers need to maximize the potential of all students.

1. COMMUNICATE WHAT YOU NEED FROM PARENTS AND STATE ALL GOALS CLEARLY.

When communicating with parents in the beginning of the year, make sure the message is clear that you need volunteers. Volunteers cannot be recruited with a signup sheet at the front of the school because it is impersonal and, thus, ineffective. Rather teachers should view themselves as recruiters. When teachers send letters or e-mails to parents, they should include a paragraph that stresses the need for volunteers and the value they possess. Before sending any letters out to parents, review them with the administration, and copy all e-mails to them as well. In the back of the book, I have placed a sample letter (Appendix A) that you are free to use. There is an old saying that the squeaky wheel gets the oil. It is time to squeak.

Also, make sure the PTA (Parent Teacher Association) is involved. If your school does not have a PTA, it may be time to have that conversation. The PTA obviously knows people in the community as well. Members can serve as a microphone to the community. Teachers should also make sure to attend PTA meetings. Though any principal can serve as a liaison, a powerful message is sent to the PTA when the principal and the teachers are speaking together with one voice.

Finally, communication does not stop. The theme that volunteers are needed should be interwoven in e-mails and school letters throughout the year. Volunteers come and go based on a myriad of circumstances. Once a volunteer is no longer able to provide his or her services, that person should be replaced without delay. Continued communication is the only way to accomplish that goal.

2. RECRUIT CHURCH CONGREGATIONS.

I don't know of a place where a greater number of potential volunteers from various professions could be found. It is a big mistake to not ask for the help of a church. A teacher has to be willing to place their own religion aside for the good of the students. I happen to be a Catholic but Cedar Creek Baptist Church was next door to Bates Elementary where I was employed. I had no problem asking for their help and their congregation was a pleasure to work with. I am also convinced that ignoring this resource would have made test scores lower.

Obviously, public schools face separation of church and state issues. The separation of church and state involves bringing religious suggestions into a public school, but it has no bearing on a church volunteer helping a struggling student with a math assignment. Teachers need to be at the forefront of this issue and answer all parental questions honestly concerning specific volunteers. Parents should also be able to meet the volunteers if they choose. Obviously, any parent who is not comfortable should be able to opt out. But a parent who does this should be made aware of the ramification of that decision. Obviously, all volunteers should be trained as well as to what they are allowed and not allowed to do. This specifically means teaching the material provided by the classroom teacher and not addressing their personal religion. The church program can fall apart quickly should a volunteer cross the line.

3. RECRUIT PROFESSIONS.

This approach is more of a short-term fix, but here's the idea: start with contacting your local law enforcement to see if a small group of off-duty officers would be willing to come out one day to help some struggling kindergarteners with their reading. Police officers are a great starting point because they are a group who are encouraged to create goodwill in the community. There should even be a sign on the outdoor bulletin board welcoming them. It could be a feel-good moment for the community at large. This kind of recognition is a good way to appreciate people and make them want to come back.

Here is the key to make this short-term fix one that may last over the course of the school year. If an officer makes a positive connection with a student, simply ask if there is another time he or she may be able to come. The connection with the student is vital. When people see that what they are doing makes a difference, it is much easier to get them to come back, even if they do not have a child in the school. The same strategy can be used for nurses, firefighters, and other professionals in the community.

The goal is to get these professionals in the building to see the positive strides the school is making and to help them understand that their personal involvement is vital to achieve the ultimate goal of the students doing their best. On a side note, if a teacher has a behaviorally challenged student who really likes fire trucks, pairing that student with a firefighter to accomplish an educational goal might be a step in the right direction. Students may hear a firefighter's motivational words in a different way from their teachers' words.

The strategies I have presented are not easy. Depending on the rules for each county, there could be many impediments to starting and maintaining a volunteer network. One hurdle, for example, could be the time it takes to get background checks. There may also be some teachers' unions who may not like church volunteers coming into schools. Overcoming obstacles takes a lot of patience. Also, the schools may not be able to mandate that teachers go along with a volunteer program, which is why it is so important for teachers to find other like-minded individuals to do what it takes to make their school the envy of others.

These ideas also take up a certain amount of time. Obviously, making various phone calls to the groups mentioned would take time outside of normal working hours. It also takes time and dedication to prepare targeted lesson plans for volunteers. Teachers have a tough job, and to implement the ideas presented in this chapter would only make it tougher. The question that needs to be addressed is whether it is worth the effort to improve the quality of education for the students.

CHAPTER 6

Pulling the Educational Bandwagon Outside of the Box

I have already talked about teachers being introspective in chapter one. I transitioned to the importance of teachers understanding what may be troubling children, motivation, expectations, and building an educational coalition. The final chapter centers on two things. The first are outside-the-box strategies to bringing in the best/most volunteers possible. New opportunities abound when the ratio of students and adults is addressed.

The second outside-the-box strategy involves technology. It is critical for teachers to know the latest material available for students and how to apply it. I have provided seven websites for teachers to use immediately. These sites contain multiple benefits for teachers and the students they serve.

The first thing I would like you to do before I get into the meat of this chapter is to play a quick game. I got this idea from a television show called *The Numbers Game,* and it really fits the purposes of this chapter. First, copy the nine dots shown below. After that, connect all nine dots by using no more than four lines. If you get too frustrated, look at Appendix B in the back of this book for the solution. Do not cheat yourself. Give this a shot before giving up.

• • •

• • •

• • •

The reason I had you do this is simple. Teachers have to understand that they have to do things differently from other teachers to differentiate themselves from those teachers. Principals want teachers who can educate students despite their home life or any other excuse. Even if the ideas from the first five chapters alone were implemented, substantial progress would be made. But what teachers should always be thinking about is how to push the envelope until the job is done.

For example, how could teachers push the envelope in terms of gaining quality volunteers? One answer is to provide times when the most parents/professionals would be available to volunteer. The majority of people have 8:00 a.m. to 5:00 p.m. jobs. Therefore, in order to attract that type of person, a school would have to go outside the box concerning when the building is typically open, such as later in the evening or on Saturday mornings. The administration must approve such an arrangement, however, because it would mean extra lights, heat, maintenance, etc. Most schools do not do this. Therefore, there will be little competition from other schools to bring strong volunteers into your school.

It is possible to have teachers who do not have small children paired with volunteers to have intense after-school sessions targeting children who need or would like to have the extra attention. It is also possible for a restaurant to agree to provide dinner for the students and volunteers in return for one week of free advertising on school grounds. For some teachers, this idea would not be feasible based on family circumstances. But for schools that have the professionals who are willing to take this leap, the hard work should be highly rewarding. One thing I have found with my own children is how rapidly they learn the material I present when distractions are limited. One evening's theme could be "polygons and pizza." Another evening could be dedicated to "timelines and tacos." Anything it takes to keep students engaged should be on the table.

Saturday morning would have the same concept. Students who come will be provided with enrichment exercises and food. This tutoring session would be a much more relaxed atmosphere than the normal school hours, but there should still be a laser-like focus on concepts teachers want students to improve upon. Business members from the community should be encouraged to attend, lay out business cards, and volunteer to read or help a child with an assignment that he or she struggled with sometime during the previous week. I will caution you, however, that schools have to be careful not to endorse any business or group.

The end goal is to have as many people as possible engaged in helping students maximize their potential. The process may not be smooth at first. Depending on your school and principal's preferences, screening, references, and command of good grammar would need to be established. But over time, as teachers and professionals know what to expect, I think you will find that there will be more volunteers than the teachers know what to do with, which is one great problem to have!

TECHNOLOGICAL "OUTSIDE THE BOX" IDEAS

I believe teachers are only in the beginning stages of how to implement technology to improve student performance. One of the game changers is the iPad. More schools are implementing this tool every year. A plethora of low-cost/free apps is available for students to use to increase learning. The cost of the iPad is still too high for many districts. Over time, price will be less of an issue.

Students using the iPad for academic purposes have an advantage over students who do not have the same opportunity. The same thinking is true when it comes to other technology. Most principals and teachers would agree that technology is important in the classroom. The ones who utilize it most effectively, however, will have the edge over other schools not using these tools to their advantage.

The following is a list of ideas meant to give teachers that technological advantage. But technology is changing all of the time. By the time schools are using these ideas, they are no longer an advantage in terms of standing out. Therefore, it is vital that teachers stay on top of the latest technological trends and determine whether they should be used in a classroom. Administrators who understand this point would be a key resource for educators. Schools that have strong technology coordinators/computer teachers also have the advantage over other schools. It is very important for teachers to do their own research but also to seek people out who may be able to give them an edge. Students are the ultimate beneficiaries of the knowledge that technology gives students access to.

1. WWW.KHANACADEMY.COM

This website was featured on *60 Minutes* on March 11, 2012. The link provided is the full show: http://www.cbsnews.com/video/watch/?id=7401696n

Khan Academy (founded by Salman Khan) is a not-for-profit company that has over 4,200 educational videos. Funding comes from the Gates Foundation and Google. The Khan Academy specializes in mathematics, but its library of material is continually growing. Khan Academy can be used on an "as-needed" basis. This resource would be great for group learning or for students to use with volunteers. Students could be assigned topics on the website for extra help on a problematic topic. The website could also be used to give extension assignments to high-performing students. The material on Khan Academy that I have researched was taught efficiently. This program is so effective that several California schools launched a pilot program to replace their current math programs.

Khan Academy is a fun and less stressful way for children to learn difficult concepts. This website is appropriate for children learning early addition all the way through advanced calculus.

One of the ways students can use Khan Academy is through the search box. For example, go to the site, and type "multiplying fractions" into the search box. You will get a tutorial on the concept with an example problem. Next, you are given the option of doing a practice problem. If a student does not understand the answer, he or she can click the area that says, "I'd like a hint." From there, further assistance is given.

2. WWW.LEARNZILLION.COM

This is a free website similar to Khan Academy in terms of the general purpose and utilization. There are several differences, however, which are worth exploring. Learnzillion.com recruited 123 teachers from 29 states. They came up with common core standards every state shares. Next, over 2,000 lessons were created based on these standards.

There are additional features on learnzillion.com not seen on Khan Academy. For example, teachers have the option of setting up their class and giving assignments directly on the website. Students receive a code in order to retrieve instructions. Assignments and quizzes have already been created in the content areas. Teachers do have to use their discretion in terms of using the assignments on the website or creating their own. Teachers can also input their grades and subject level. The standards are provided for the teacher.

Another difference between learnzillion.com and Khan Academy is that learnzillion.com has reading assignments for grades third through eighth. Reading assignments are not an option on Khan Academy.

Both Learnzillion.com and Khan Academy are valuable resources. Material is presented in unique ways that are valuable for students with different learning styles. Teachers should check out both websites and determine which one they find most beneficial.

3. WWW.EDUCATIONWORLD.COM

This website, like the others, is free. It addresses a wide variety of educational resources in several subject areas. The website contains lessons along with links to numerous other educational websites. I like educationworld.com because of all the subjects covered and the lesson plans. One problem is that the subjects are not divided by grade or core content specific to a teacher's state. Therefore, it can take a little more time to find the material needed.

Educationworld.com can also be used for students who are struggling or to give extension assignments to those who have tested highly on a pretest for a given unit. Education World has a neat feature called Learning Machine Games. They are games in the areas of math, reading, and science. I would use this to reinforce concepts in a fun manner.

One of the many games is called *Wild Weather Adventure*. The game can be played with one to four players. Players have to spin a virtual wheel that takes them to places all over the globe. From there, the student answers an easy, medium, or hard question about weather. The game is educational and will keep the attention of students.

One of the objections I have to this website is toward the bottom of the site. It's a tab called "This Week in Education." Controversial topics in education are listed. Therefore, I would not allow a child to use this without the supervision of an adult who has been trained on the website.

4. WWW.EDMODO.COM

Edmodo.com has lots of valuable functions, and they are all free of charge. For example, teachers can connect with other teachers from all over the world in the subject areas they choose. But there is also a filtering device so that teachers can receive messages only from the people they choose.

Virtual classrooms are created by teachers who give students a code. Once the students log in, they can create their unique usernames and passwords. Students can be given assignments and timed quizzes, or teachers can answer students' questions. Parents also get a code they can use to monitor their children's activity and check on their progress.

Teachers can upload assignments to Edmodo, or they can create assignments directly on the website. From there, each assignment can be sent to the entire class, a small group, or individuals. This gives the teacher flexibility to ensure that all students are learning on their particular level. There is also a grade book on the site, which saves valuable time.

Another great feature is that a teacher can link to videos. For example, if a teacher wanted to give an assignment on multiplying fractions, he or she could choose to link to a small lesson from the Khan Academy's website. The student would click on the link, watch the video, and complete the teacher's assignment.

The teacher also has the option of what type of quiz questions he or she wants to give. A teacher can choose any combination of multiple choice, true/false, fill in the blank, matching, or short-answer questions.

One drawback to Edmodo is that it takes time to get used to the various functions of the website. Class time would need to be used to introduce children to the features on the site. Finally, some children may not have internet access at home. Therefore, that child could not be expected to complete homework assigned on Edmodo.

5. WWW.GOOGLE.COM/EARTH/INDEX.HTML

Google Earth is a terrific free site that allows students and teachers to see pictures and/or videos of regions they are studying. There are also tutorials on the site that I highly recommend. For example, a teacher who is working on a science unit involving trees can use Google Earth to study fifty different types of trees from all over the world using their 3-D images.

According to one of the tutorials on the website, a teacher can also record a customized tour of locations with voiceovers. Teachers can use this powerful tool in many ways. For example, if a teacher were teaching the difference between mountains and plains, he or she could record locations of each along with the intricate aspects of each, giving students powerful visuals that cannot be gathered from a textbook.

Google Earth can also be used to study the solar system. With one click of a mouse, a teacher can switch views from the earth to the sky. Mars can be studied in great detail. Have a class studying the moon? A teacher can use Google Earth to show the class a virtual tour of the moon by astronaut Buzz Aldrin.

The possibilities of this site are vast. It is worth a teacher's time to check it out and utilize the material.

6. WWW.SKYPE.COM

This is a free phone/video service that can be used to connect teachers from other schools in order to discuss various educational issues, including lesson planning, discipline, and assessments. The concept here is to link teachers in order to develop a professional learning community. Teachers' time and gas money are saved with this solution. All that is required is a webcam and an internet connection. There is even a low-cost feature that allows group video calls for up to ten people. With the extra time saved by not having to travel to other schools, a teacher may choose to use that time to plan lessons.

7. WWW.STUDYISLAND.COM

Studyisland.com is a paid service, so teachers may want to schedule a demo with the company to see whether the product would be right for them and then present it to their principals. In essence, studyisland.com is similar to learnzillion.com in the sense that the activities created are based on the standards in each state. But there are differences.

Studyisland.com is self-paced instruction based on games and rewards. Core content in math, reading, writing, science, and social studies is covered. A neat feature is that a teacher can receive real-time data on a student's progress. Statistical data on the studyisland. com website illustrates its impact on students, which was impressive.

I will caution teachers that I live in a large county where many teachers use studyisland.com. A simplification of a report I discovered showed that improvement was made, but it was not statistically significant. The county is going to continue with the program and further evaluate the impact on students. The bottom of this paragraph has the link to that report. Teachers can also Google "study island jcps" for the website. I will give Study Island a pass for now because the program is new in the district where I live. It is possible that teachers needed more training on this website or to use the website more effectively to get the most out of it. http://www.jefferson.k12.ky.us/Departments/Planning/ProgramEvaluation/SuccMaker_StdIsleEval5813DD.pdf

Technology was once an afterthought in educating students. That mind-set has to change. Teachers must integrate technology into the daily lives of students inside and outside of the classroom. I completely sympathize with teachers who have taught many years and are having a hard time moving away from traditional educational techniques. But technology in our society is changing quickly and is here to stay. Those who do not change with it are doing a disservice to their students.

FINAL THOUGHTS

One question that has not been fully addressed in this book is *why*?

Why should a teacher invest in the effort to improve skills when spending the time to do does not garner any additional income? Why should teachers work so hard outside the classroom with students whose parents do not put in the maximum effort to have their children succeed? Shouldn't there be some accountability on their part? Why should educators put in the extra time working with and training volunteers when they could simply go home or spend that time working on lesson plans?

These are tough questions. I have only two answers.

My first answer revolves around the reason many teachers entered the profession in the first place: because they love working with children and desire to see them succeed. There was an old comedy film back in the eighties called *Summer School*. The main character, played by Mark Harmon, was asked by his principal about teaching summer school. He replied that he got into the teaching gig to "have his summers off." Although the line was funny in the movie, it is a sad state of affairs to get into a profession based on when a person will *not* be working.

Most of the teachers I have had the privilege of working with did not have that attitude. They were hardworking professionals who wanted only the best for their students. Unfortunately, situations would come along that impeded their progress. It could be a discipline problem in the classroom, pressure from administrators about test scores, or a feeling of frustration because students were not performing despite their best efforts. I understand that circumstances can be difficult, but, hopefully, the ideas in this book will continue to help fuel teachers' flames.

The second answer to the question of why, for me, is based on my experiences with two girls, Brandi and Alexis. I taught both children as second graders. They were two of the brightest children I have had the pleasure of working with. Recently, I was cleaning my office when I found an old envelope addressed to me. It was from Brandi. It included a picture and an invitation to her fifth grade graduation. At this point, I was two years removed from teaching and was absolutely floored. I decided to go and was fortunate enough to sit by her parents. We shared some great memories and had a wonderful time.

Afterwards, there was a reception in the cafeteria. I said hello to many of my former colleagues and students. There was a child, however, who was staring at me from a short distance. Once I focused on her, I knew it was Alexis. I went over to say hi but was a bit cautious because it appeared that she was trying to process who I was. I bent toward her and asked if she remembered me. Alexis dropped her head a bit. When she looked back up, she started to cry. It was one of the most touching moments I had ever shared with a child who was not my own.

Therefore, the second answer to why when it comes to teaching and doing the extra work is that some students will never forget it. They will remember only certain teachers well. Typically, the teachers who have the biggest impact on their students are the ones remembered most fondly. I remember teachers like that, and the odds are that all of you who are reading this do as well.

Now that you have finished this book, I hope I have fulfilled my goal. I wanted to inspire teachers while providing concrete answers to some of the professions most difficult challenges. I wish nothing but success on your journey.

APPENDIX A

Sample Volunteering Letter to Parents

Dear parents,

As you are keenly aware, (Success Elementary) has been working hard to create the best possible learning environment for your child. Our teachers come into the building early and work late because of the vested interest we have in seeing your child succeed.

After studying the data, it is apparent that our school can do more, and this is where you come in. It has been determined that, despite our teacher's best efforts, they cannot be everywhere at once. Certain students learn more efficiently when one-on-one time is given.

We have so many students at (Success Elementary) who need only a little push to get to the next level. We have B students who need a little more attention to become A students. We have C students who, with your help, can earn that coveted B average. We also have some students who are failing. Even with these students, the potential is there for educational breakthroughs by giving them the additional attention they need.

Our goal is to have the highest volunteer rate of any school in the county. We understand that some of you have time conflicts, which is why we are starting a "volunteer on the run" program. This program is geared toward busy professionals who have precious little time to spare. We have quick enrichment lessons and students who are ready to learn. All we need is a small block of time from you to help a child with a concept he or she has not yet mastered. The lesson could involve something as easy as addition and subtraction problems. We will match you with the subjects you feel are your best.

Those of you who have more time to give can help children on a set schedule of your choosing. These sessions will have a relaxed atmosphere. For example, we are planning a Saturday morning Doughnuts with Dads enrichment session. This event will focus on dads who can come in and work on an educational concept with a child (such as reading or math) while eating a tasty treat. More details will be coming soon!

Our school is so excited to take education to the next level. With your help, we will be the leaders in educational advancement. All students at (Success Elementary) have the potential to benefit from your time and efforts. Thank you in advance for all of your hard work and dedication to our school and students. A follow-up form/e-mail will be sent to assess how many parents we can get to help, which program suits you the best, and to provide sign up opportunities.

Sincerely,
Clayton Thomas

APPENDIX B

Solution to Connecting the Dots Using Only Four Lines

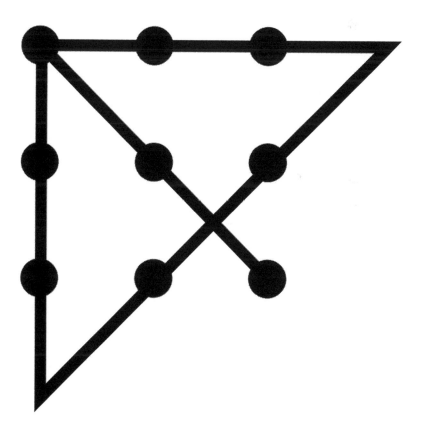

This picture was taken from Ask.com. The key is to go
outside the box created by your mind with the lines.

CONTACT PAGE

I can be found at http://www.beyondthelessonplans.com. I look forward to clarifying any details in this book. I am also available to speak at your school and answer all questions.

21814727R00056

Made in the USA
San Bernardino, CA
07 June 2015